**Imitating** *Nature*

# From Bug Legs to
# Walking Robots

Other books in this series include:

# Imitating *Nature*

# From Bug Legs to Walking Robots

**Toney Allman**

**KIDHAVEN PRESS**

*An imprint of Thomson Gale, a part of The Thomson Corporation*

THOMSON

GALE

Detroit • New York • San Francisco • San Diego • New Haven, Conn. • Waterville, Maine • London • Munich

For more information, contact
KidHaven Press
27500 Drake Rd.
Farmington Hills, MI 48331-3535
Or you can visit our Internet site at http://www.gale.com

**LIBRARY OF CONGRESS CATALOGING-IN-PUBLICATION DATA**

Allman, Toney.
  From bug legs to walking robots/ by Toney Allman.
    p. cm. — (Imitating nature)
  Includes bibliographical references and index.
  ISBN 0-7377-3385-3 (hard cover : alk. paper)

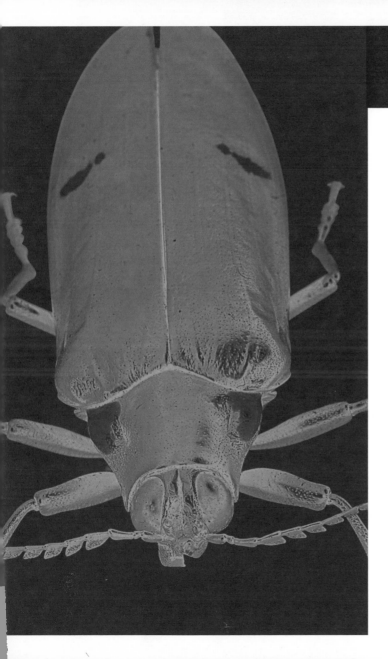

# Contents

# CHAPTER 1

# The Power of Many Legs

Millions upon millions of creepy, crawly creatures live on Earth. They are **arthropods**, or animals such as insects, crickets, centipedes, and spiders that have six, eight, even dozens of legs. Scientists are fascinated by these creatures because of their special **locomotion** abilities. They move from place to place with ease. They can skitter, climb, jump, and scurry into places people and their machines cannot go.

If scientists could invent robots that move as easily as arthropods do, these robots could go places that wheeled robots and humans cannot. This is just what some scientists did. However, first they had to learn exactly how creatures with many legs walk and run.

## Arthropod Legs

Arthropods do not have legs that stick straight down, as horses or people do. Instead, their legs sprawl out from their bodies. Each leg is made up of several

*Opposite: A magnified image shows a centipede crawling with ease on its many legs. The green weevil (inset) is just as graceful on its six legs.*

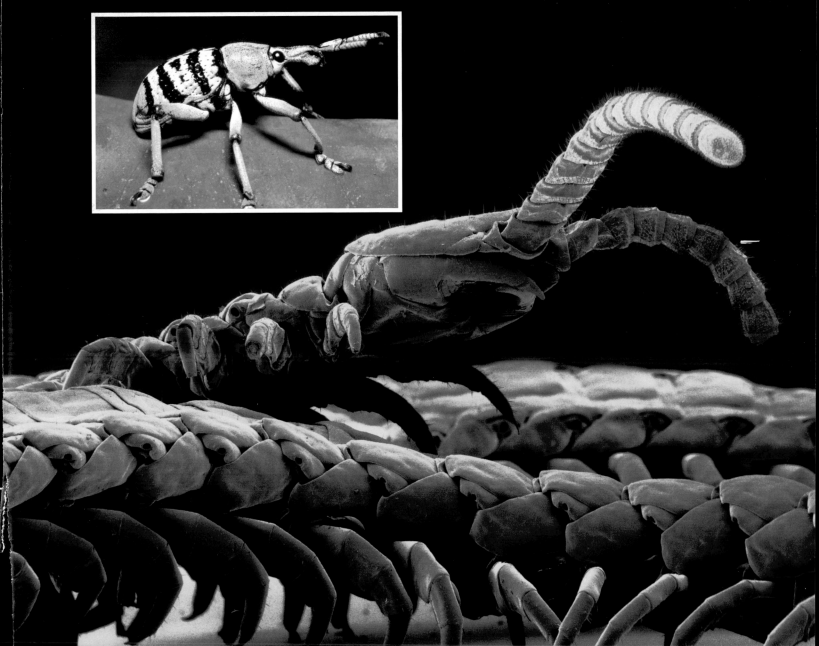

parts, or **segments**. Each segment is **jointed** so that it can move or bend in different directions. The legs are attached to the body by a round joint, similar to a human's shoulder joint. From these joints, the legs come out from the sides of the body and point upward before bending down to the ground. An arthropod's legs are so thin and weak that they have to point upward, like a lever, to hold up the body. Yet even without strength, arthropod legs can do amazing things.

A cockroach, for instance, is an insect with six sprawled legs. With these six legs some cockroaches can run 3.4 miles (5.5km) an hour. That means a cockroach can run fifty times its body length in one second. If people could run fifty of their body lengths in a second, they could run 200 miles (300km) an hour!

Its legs also keep the cockroach very **stable** when it is standing, walking, running, or climbing. A cockroach is hard to knock over no matter where it goes or what it is doing. Six sprawled legs do not have the strength of a horse's legs, for example. They cannot race at high speed while carrying a load. However, a

*Like all arthropods, this colorful beetle has extremely flexible legs that sprawl out from its body.*

From Bug Legs to Walking Robots

# Fast and Sturdy

## How a Roach Uses Its Legs to Run and Stay Balanced

**1** The cockroach has six flexible legs that sprawl out from its body. They give the roach a wide base of support and make it a fast runner.

**2** To run, the roach springs forward with three legs, and balances on the other three legs.

**3** The roach rapidly shuffles its legs forward and back, making sure to keep three feet on the ground at a time.

**4** The roach's ability to use three legs for running and three legs for balance allows it to quickly cross difficult terrain and never trip or fall.

Legs for Running

Legs for Balance

fast-running horse that steps in a hole is in danger of falling or breaking a leg. A cockroach is never bothered by dangers such as holes. Its legs give it a wide base of support, and it does not slip or fall.

## Flexible and Useful

Thin, sprawled arthropod legs have other benefits, too. Spiders have eight legs, and each leg has seven segments. So many segments mean a spider's legs can bend in many more ways than people's legs can. With its superbendable legs, a spider can crawl across its web, even upside down, with no trouble at all.

Having many legs gives arthropods another advantage. While standing on their middle and back legs, bugs often use their front two legs for grabbing, fighting, or eating. Some centipedes, for example, have 44 legs. The two back legs have little pincers on them that snap at anything that attacks from the rear. The front two legs have claws that can deliver a painful poison to an enemy. Many arthropods can use their two front legs as tools or arms while they stand steadily on their remaining legs. Praying mantises, for example, have

*Fighting for dominance, two stag beetles lock their pincers and flail their front legs at each other.*

## The World's Greatest Weightlifter

**For their size, rhinoceros beetles are the strongest creatures in the world. These insects can walk for half an hour carrying a load on their backs that is 30 times their own weight. If humans could do this, they could walk a mile carrying a Cadillac.**

*For its size, the rhinoceros beetle is the strongest creature on the planet.*

two huge front legs that grab and kill insects. Even when holding a big, struggling grasshopper, the mantis is well-balanced on its other four legs.

## A Buggy Notion

Scientists wanted to build robots with all the abilities of arthropods. Putting six legs on a robot was not enough. They had to know what qualities of the legs to copy so that robots could do what bugs do— speed around in all sorts of places, use their legs as tools, and explore without ever getting stuck, breaking down, or falling over. At the University of California, in Berkeley, Robert Full set up his Poly-PEDAL Laboratory to figure out the secrets of arthropod locomotion and help other scientists invent robots that move like bugs.

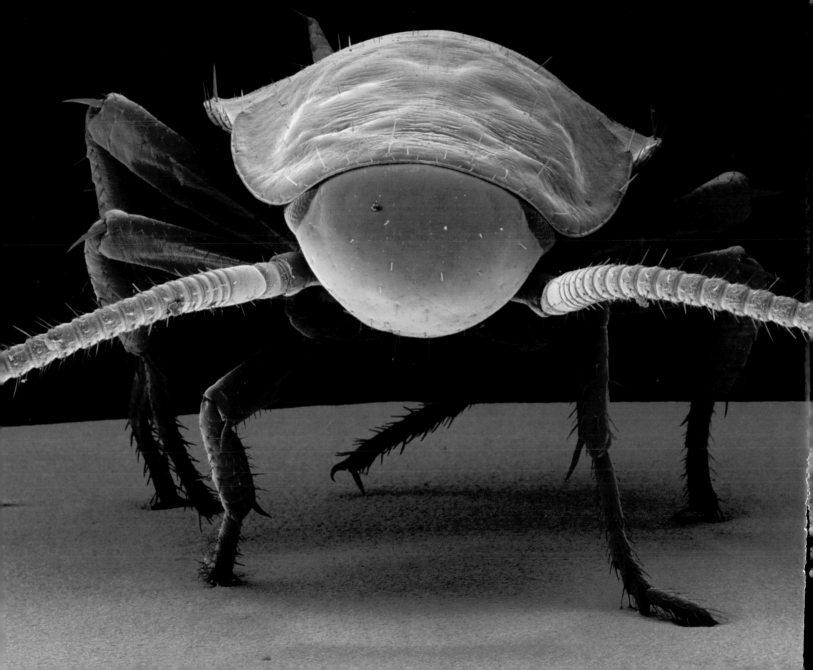

# CHAPTER 2

# Welcome to Bug Land

Robert Full's lab is like a gym where bugs do exercises, take tests, and show off their skills. The arthropods have taught Full some fascinating facts about the locomotion of many legs.

Full already knew how people and four-legged animals move. When people or animals such as horses run, they bounce along as if their legs are pogo sticks. Wheeled machines, on the other hand, move smoothly with no springy motion. Many scientists thought that bugs must move smoothly, like wheeled machines. They thought having many sprawled legs must be like having wheels. Full decided to find out if this was true.

## In the Insect Gym

Full smeared a thin layer of flavored gelatin on a well-lighted platform. He put centipedes on the surface of the gelatin so that he could see the footprint

*Opposite: The cockroach, shown here highly magnified, is one of the many arthropods that Robert Full studies in his lab.*

trail they made as they ran. Instead of running, the centipedes ate the gelatin. Full decided to switch to plain, unflavored gelatin instead. Then the centipedes ran across the track, and each footstep sank slightly into the gelatin. A light flashed under the surface wherever a footstep poked into the thin gelatin. Full recorded every step of every leg to see how centipedes moved.

*During one of Full's experiments, a flash of light (close-up, inset) appears where a centipede steps in gelatin.*

Then Full built a little bug treadmill. It was a continuous loop of moving track inside a clear box. Full put cockroaches and centipedes on the treadmill and took their pictures as they ran. He used cameras that took a thousand pictures a second. This way he could see the tiniest details of how their legs moved.

# Like a Three-Legged Stool

When Full saw the results of all his experiments, he was surprised. Bugs walk and run just as other animals and people do, not like smooth wheels. The joints in the bugs' legs make them springy, and each leg bounces along like a pogo stick.

Full discovered that bugs that have many legs can bounce along steadily because almost all of them run with a **tripod gait**. This means that two legs on one side of the body and one leg on the other side stay on the ground while another three legs lift up and move forward. This is true for cockroaches, which have six legs. It is also true of centipedes, with 44 legs. Groups of legs at the front, in the middle, and at the rear form tripods for centipedes. Three bug legs work as one human leg or two horse legs work. Two legs, four legs, six legs—even dozens of legs—all run and bounce with the same kind of motion.

*To study centipede movement in detail, Full takes high-speed pictures of a centipede running on a treadmill.*

## What Good Are Many Legs?

Full wondered what advantages many legs with a tripod gait had over two or four legs for staying stable. Bugs did not run differently than other animals. Why did they need many legs?

Full built a tiny, bumpy obstacle course. Then he watched how fast cockroaches could run through it. Tripod gaits proved their value on the obstacle course. Full discovered that creatures with many legs such as cockroaches never stumbled when they ran on bumpy surfaces. Animals with two or four legs could not have run such a course without falling or at least slowing down. Cockroaches could speed right along. They could climb obstacles three times their height, race across miniature ditches, and turn tight

### Yucky but Cool

Full studies bugs, but he is not crazy about them. He once told a reporter, "I personally think cockroaches are repulsive. But you don't have to like them to find them interesting."

*A scientist inserts electrode wires into the legs of a cockroach in order to study the insect's leg muscles.*

corners. Tripod gaits are what make bugs so steady and stable.

## Like a Rock

To find out just how stable cockroaches are, Full next stuck tiny cannons on their backs. He shot them off to see how much pressure it took to knock the bugs over. When the cannons exploded, the cockroaches stumbled. Before the smoke cleared, however, their springy legs were back to running as fast as ever. No wheeled machine or horse could ever have done that. Having many legs and tripod gaits makes bugs tough, sturdy athletes that do not fall down.

## Bug Inspiration

Now scientists understood how to build legs as steady and stable as arthropod legs. Full's experiments showed exactly why bug legs work so well. Some inspired scientists decided to build robots with sprawled, jointed, bouncy legs that would walk with a tripod gait. If these scientists were skillful, they could build in other bug-leg advantages, too.

*With its six legs and tripod gait, the cockroach is one of the most sure-footed arthropods.*

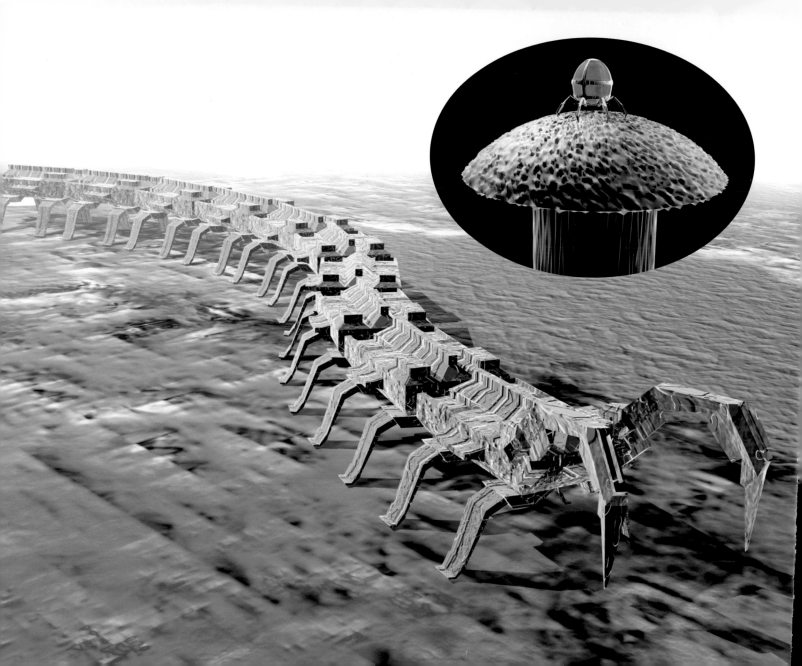

# CHAPTER 3

# Tiny Robots Inspired by Nature

In laboratories around the United States, scientists have built tiny robots inspired by spiders and cockroaches. They are not yet as fast, strong, or small as real bugs, but their legs mimic arthropod locomotion.

## iSprawl

Robert Full helped Mark Cutkosky and his team at Stanford University in California build cockroach robots. In 2003 their robot, named iSprawl, was born. It has a plastic body, six sprawled jointed legs, complicated wiring, an electric motor, and a tiny computer that controls its legs. It runs on batteries.

iSprawl is about 4.5 inches (115mm) long and weighs 11 ounces (315g). It is larger than a real cockroach but small enough to fit in a person's hand. With its computer guided legs, iSprawl can scamper down the street without human control. It can run fifteen times its body length in one second.

*Opposite: A computer illustration shows a tiny mechanical centipede and a microscopic spiderlike robot on the head of a pin (inset).*

19

## If It Breaks . . .

A big advantage of bug robots is that they are inexpensive to build. iSprawl, for example, is built with parts that cost about $1,300. Spiderbots can be built for about $600. Inexpensive robots are best for missions in dangerous places. If they get blown up or break down, they can be replaced easily.

The best thing about iSprawl is that it is tough, stable, and bounces along like a pogo stick. With its tripod gait, it can crawl over obstacles as high as its belly and not fall over. Someday, roach robots such as iSprawl will work in dangerous places such as disaster areas. They will climb through rubble and search for survivors in buildings destroyed by earthquakes or tsunamis. Tough and fast as a cockroach, iSprawls will go where people and wheeled robots cannot.

## Mini-Whegs™

Cutkosky is not the only scientist building bug robots. Roger Quinn builds Mini-Whegs in his Biologically Inspired Robotics Laboratory at Case Western Reserve University in Ohio. Mini-Whegs are 3.5 inches (9cm) long and have both legs and wheels. They can run ten body lengths per second and climb stairs and ramps.

Each Mini-Whegs has four wheels with three legs attached to each wheel. The wheels are for moving fast. The legs are for climbing. Mini-Whegs improve on nature by having two ways to move. They may someday do search-and-rescue work or clear minefields for the military.

From Bug Legs to Walking Robots

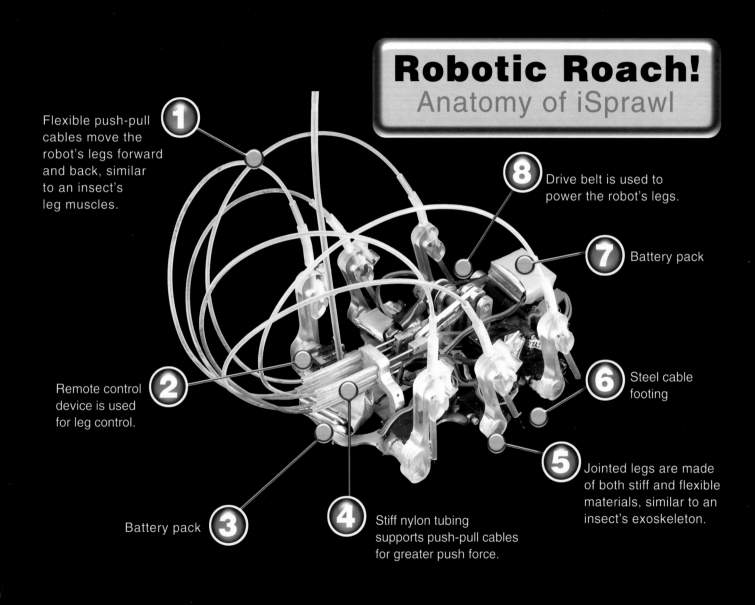

**Robotic Roach!**
Anatomy of iSprawl

1 Flexible push-pull cables move the robot's legs forward and back, similar to an insect's leg muscles.

8 Drive belt is used to power the robot's legs.

7 Battery pack

2 Remote control device is used for leg control.

6 Steel cable footing

3 Battery pack

4 Stiff nylon tubing supports push-pull cables for greater push force.

5 Jointed legs are made of both stiff and flexible materials, similar to an insect's exoskeleton.

*A Mini-Whegs uses its wheel-legs to climb over a board.*

# Spider-Bots

At the National Aeronautics and Space Administration (NASA) Jet Propulsion Laboratory (JPL) in California, Robert Hogg and his research team have invented spider-bots. NASA and JPL want spider-bots to explore Mars or comets. They want tiny robots that can crawl into tight places on space stations to do repairs. The first spider-bot, named Yosi, was built in 2002. Although Yosi is called a spider-bot, it has only six jointed legs. Yosi is 7 inches (18cm) tall and weighs 14 ounces (400g). It has tiny artificial muscles, camera eyes, and two long feelers that sense obstacles ahead. It has a little computer brain that directs its leg movements. A person chooses its path by remote control.

Yosi used its tough, stable tripod gait in JPL's Mars Yard. The Mars Yard is a big sandbox, about 98 feet (30m) square, filled with rocks of different sizes. Yosi walked in the soft sand without getting stuck. It

Below: Spyder was one of the first insect-inspired robots. Right: Built in 2000, Ariel is a sophisticated crab robot that searches for mines on the seafloor.

squeezed between large rocks and crawled over small ones without crashing into anything.

In 2004, JPL built another spider-bot with an extra leg that works like an arm. This spider-bot can build a tower with toy logs all by itself. The JPL team also invented a spider-bot called the Web-crawler that can crawl on a wire mesh, just like a spider on its web. It crawls across the wire with a tripod gait. It can even walk across its web upside down.

In the future, NASA and JPL plan to build hundreds of spider-bots that can explore space. They will have six, eight, or even eighty legs, depending on the jobs they need to do. The legs will

*Although bug robots like the iSprawl may look like toys, they are actually complex machines designed to carry out important missions.*

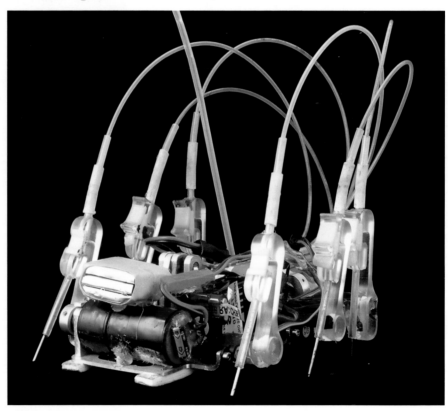

From Bug Legs to Walking Robots

be replaceable, with different kinds of tools for digging, repairing, and doing experiments.

# Here They Come!

Mini-Whegs, iSprawls, and spider-bots look like toys, but they all have serious roles to play in the future. Many scientists believe that the 21st century will be the century of robots. Bug robots are rapidly becoming tougher, faster, smaller, and smarter. Soon they will leave their lab homes and scurry into everyday life.

## Robot Skin

Today bug robots run on batteries that have to be replaced every few hours. In the future, JPL scientists plan to design an artificial skin for spider-bots that can absorb energy from the Sun and never run out of power. With a longer battery life, spider-bots could tackle long-term missions.

# Glossary

**arthropods:** Hard-shelled animals without backbones that have pairs of jointed legs. Crabs, insects, and spiders are examples of arthropods.

**jointed:** Having joints, which are points along the arthropod leg where moving parts join.

**locomotion:** The act of moving from place to place, such as walking or running.

**segments:** Sections of a jointed leg.

**stable:** Maintaining balance and not easily moved or disturbed.

**tripod gait:** A means of locomotion in which two legs on one side of the body and one leg on the opposite side are on the ground at any one time. This is the way almost all arthropods walk and run.

# For Further Exploration

## Books

Roger Bridgman, *Robot* New York: DK Eyewitness, 2004. From the first primitive robots to the complex thinking machines of today, this book examines robots in all their forms and through all their jobs. Learn how difficult and complicated designing a robot can be.

Clive Gifford, *How to Build a Robot*. Danbury, CT: Franklin Watts, 2000. This fun book, complete with cartoons, briefly describes the history of robots, explains some basic robotic principles, and compares robots, computers, and human brains. Read about the earliest efforts to build robots with many legs that did not turn out very well.

Theresa Greenway, *Big Book of Bugs*. New York: DK, 2000. Bugs of every description come alive in the pages of this book. Discover fascinating facts about spiders, insects, caterpillars, and more. Big color photographs accompany the text.

Claire Llewellyn, *I Didn't Know That Spiders Have Fangs* Brookfield, CT: Copper Beech, 1997. The best human efforts cannot come close to the amazing capabilities of real spiders. In this easy-to-read book, learn about the fascinating talents of different spiders. Meet spiders that jump, spit, dance, and, of course, weave marvelous webs.

## Web Sites

**NASA Space Place** (http://spaceplace.nasa.gov/en/kids/mu.html). Explore this Web site to find out about NASA's work with robots. There are projects and puzzles, too.

**Sprawl Robots** (www-cdr.stanford.edu/biomimetics/documents/sprawl). Take a look at iSprawl's family tree. Many Sprawl robots were developed and improved upon before iSprawl joined the family. There are even bug robot movies to see, one in Sprawl-o-vision!

**The Tech: Robotics** (www.thetech.org/robotics/universal/index.htm). This huge site for kids describes all kinds of robots, in history and in modern life. Meet Robo Tuna, the Mars rovers, and robots that walk on two legs.

**Yahooligans! Animals: Insects** (http://yahooligans.yahoo.com/content/animals/insects). Explore the characteristics and behaviors of hundreds of different bugs on this large site.

**Yucky Roach World** (http://yucky.kids.discovery.com/no flash/roaches). Learn lots of amazing cockroach facts with your reporter, Wendell Worm.

# Index

# Picture Credits

# About the Author

Toney Allman holds degrees from Ohio State University and the University of Hawaii. She currently lives on the Chesapeake Bay of Virginia and cannot wait to buy her own personal bug robot.